MINDFUL RHAPSODY

POEMS

IRENE SEDEORA

In memory of Ralph and Pearl Richeson

ACKNOWLEDGMENTS

Across the Border, *The New Moon Review*.
Before the Pickup, *Bound*.
Christmas Dinner, *The Romance Rag*.
Cocoon, *Parting Gifts*.
Happy Birthday World, *The Sunday Suitor*
Homemade Lemonade, *The Florida Villager*.
Inheritance, *The Aurorean*.
In San Francisco, *ESC! Magazine*.
Kate Smith Sings Subterranean, *Second Glance; HA! Magazine*.
Lost in Puerto Rico, *The Bluffs*.
Make Over, *The Mid-America Poetry Review*.
Mango, *Limestone Circle*.
Moonflower, *Voices Along the River*.
Newborn, *PoeTalk, Our Bundle of Joy*, Meadowbrook Press.
Night in New Orleans, *Ibbetson Street Press*.
Oak to Oak, *Procreation*.
Oasis, *Ariel*.
Old Rock and Roll Stars, *Northern Ohio Live*.
Paradise, *The Catbird Seat*.
Reading Marilyn's Mail, *H.A.K.T.U.P.*
Renovation, *The Earth as Home*, Milkweed website.
Revisit to the Old Neighborhood, *Dust & Fire*.
Siren, *The Guild*.
Slow Poet, *The Writer*.
Stopping in Oklahoma City, *The TMP Irregular*.
Stuck in Traffic, *Love Poems for the Media Age*, Ripple Effect Press.
Submerged, *H.A.K.T.U.P. Fluid Ink Press*.
Summer Night, *Poe Talk*.
Sundae, *The Blue Collar Review, Footsteps*, and *Working Hard for the Money*.
Supper, *ESC! Magazine*.
Tableau of Nature, *Smorgasbord Poetry Journal*.
This Tuesday Morning, *The TMP Irregular*.
Trick or Treat Triolet, *Hazmat Review*.
Late November, *Ibid*.
Tanka, *Idiom*.
The Only Place Open, *Yet Another Small Magazine*.
The View from my Perch, *Isosceles*.
The Waitress at the Waffle Shop, *Good Foot Magazine, The Griffin*, and *Working Hard for the Money*, Bottom Dog Press.
This Manhattan Morning, *Idiom*.
Tourist, *Rearview Quarterly*.
Two Haiku, *Ha! Magazine*.

Table of Contents

Lost in Puerto Rico

We went for a drive in Puerto Rico
Searching for the resort where
James Bond roamed casino tables
Armed with a Beretta and a stiletto heeled siren.
On a cliff above the sea we found the oasis
In the sun a gleaming jewel.
We played the slots and lost
Then sat on a terrace
Pretending we were rich
Drinking margaritas
Until the sun slipped down, a flaming yoyo
That sent ribbons across the dark water.
The only Spanish words in my fuzzy mind:
Hola, gracias, buenos dias.
'We should go,' I said, as I glanced at the inky sky.
'What if we get lost?'
In a strange neighborhood stray dogs
Barked at our slow moving rental
As we crept from stop sign to stop sign
No maps, no GPS just us and our foolishness
Fear mounting as behind, blue lights suddenly
Flashed *STOP!* No one knew we were here,
If we disappeared like a ripple in the sea
To become a headline: *Lost in Puerto Rico.*
We followed the blue lights back to the highway,
Thanked the youthful cop and headed back to safety
  and our hotel bed,
    dreamed on.

The Waitress at the Waffle Shop

Like a country singer
her voice twangs and the scent of breakfast
infuses the air.
With her prattle she pours coffee
as cursorily as she mixed
a bloody Mary at Nick's,
the last place she worked.

In a voice full of grit
the waitress at the Waffle Shop
calls orders to the cook, then scatters
her life to the pair
perched at the counter.
I moved up here to have a life.
But I miss the beaches. I'm thirty-nine and
I never got married. It's just me and my dog.

The two aged birds munching waffles
        nibble up
                every word.

A Pianissimo Escape

I recall a vase of fanning feathers
plucked from a peacock and the elephant table
entwined with leaves of silk.
The hands of 3 wooden monkeys warned me
of seeing, hearing or speaking evil.
And in an aura of fame
the photos of movie stars hung silver framed.

In a room of exotica
when I was twelve
each Tuesday after school
I spent three quarters of an hour
seated at Mrs. Eddy's piano.

Above the spinet, a mirror reflected me
and my guru. She called me *Girlie*.

Sometimes she sat alongside me
across the keys her fingers festinating-
perfection I could never replay.

For a year I struggled to conquer scales,
Fur Elise and more. And then
my interest wisped away
            in a pianissimo escape.

Tanka

Rainwater lingers
In the gutter, doves pecking
Febrile afternoon
Aviary troubadours
Their voracity quenching

Failure to Yield

From across the street he watched me
that summer I was sixteen.
I did not lift my eyes from the grass
whispering to ignore him

until my hand reached past pink roses
and opened the mailbox, determined
his gaze would not deter me
that sultry season

when I dreamed of escape.
A supermarket circular flamed:
Strawberries, 2 quarts for the price of 1!
With temerity he called to me

but I studied the flyer like it was a map
and he was compelled to toss again his oily quip-
Did you get a letter from him today?
It's none of your business, I said to the dandelion

before my sandal crushed its yellow head.
Hell, I'll make it my business, he yelled
and down the street he hot-rodded
a bad muffler rattling his discontent.

a greasy hors d'oeuvre

don't whistle. i don't want your attention, as i walk past the factory with its open windows. i'm not trying to attract your interest. i just want to reach my destination, the bus stop. at sixteen and on my way to high school, it's not easy being cute—not in this place i want to escape. if i keep my eyes focused straight ahead and think of the midmorning exam, maybe you'll ignore me. after the long winter i have shed my parka and boots, announcing now my figure, fit beneath the pleated skirt, the peter pan collar ascending over the sweater like twin crescent moons. my feet are supported by penny loafers, my ankles snug inside sport socks. on the opposite side of the street, carrying books and my hope to be invisible with my quick steps, i scurry past. suddenly from an open window a man launches his testosterone call, slicing the april air with his gender. ignoring the hi honey he tosses to me like a greasy hors d'oeuvre, i hurry on.

Practicing

At sixteen, my sister became Julia Child.
even now the mystery remains
why she chose apple pie to perfect
over lemon meringue.

or chocolate cream
that long ago July day
the brawny scent of apples
filled our kitchen.

I remember how she stopped
to pin up her flyaway hair
the apron she wore
blue gingham dusted with Gold Medal

upon its bib the stain of cherries
or was it black berries?
Into the blue-rimmed bowl
she sifted flour mountains, mashed lard
hard. The pastry caused trouble and
damn dough, damn dough became her mantra.

On a trivet amid table clutter
2 apple pies cooled
sugar bubbles erupting pastry crowns
like golden lava. I remember how
she wouldn't let us taste any
until Daddy got home.

Kate Smith Sings Subterranean

In Carlsbad Caverns

One Fourth of July

She placed her Rubenesque shape

Among back lit stalactites and

Stalagmites and sang

Her rendition

Of God Bless America

Causing a thousand dreaming

 Bats to shiver

 In ecstasy.

Inheritance

Emitting the scent of cologne
Mother's stone heavy pocketbook
spills onto the kitchen table its treasures:
pills held prisoner under letters of the week
safety pins chained in togetherness
the billfold bulging photos
a jangle of coins, scissors and a screwdriver
crinkled greenbacks in small denominations
the bill from a baby Bell, letters from Texas
her wristwatch wound down
a rabbit's foot run

    out
        of
           luck.

Past eyelet curtains, the breeze whispers
to grown up siblings

    Still I love you.

Supper

A pinch of this
with a dash of that

in the scarlet sauce
that Mama stirred

as the savory scents
enhanced with love

effused from the kitchen
and into the street.

Dancing into the sky
a delightful savor-

      lent to the horizon.

Sundae

Something sensual
the way he spoons
ice cream, the youth

behind the counter.
Something naughty,
the way he pours

warm chocolate,
and jets the cream.
Something fiery

the way his knife
halves a cherry.
Enjoy, he says,

      with a wink.

The View from my Perch

In the coffee shop
Through plate glass:
Three feathered bodies
Flamboyant in November drizzle.

Slow Day, their beaks seem to say
These elders, fat and squawky
As behind the kiosk
They waddle in the quiet morning.
Nearby no pool side sunbathers
No one to buy Hernando's sarongs
Or visors that shout Florida in Day-Glo letters.
Raindrop damp three parrots
A jolt of green and pink
Three aviary Sophia Tuckers

Amid lush growth
Behind the grass roofed hut
Blurred by raindrops.
In Orlando, a moistened Monet day.

Submerged

A glint of opal
Old gold and

Aquamarine
Weaving relics.

Like fluid jewels
Fishes ransack

History's incident
Their fins brushing

This watery home
Built by happenstance.

Remnants of a staircase
Nudged by coral crusted plates

Marooned here
In bottles still corked

Vintage wine
Chilled for a buffet

That never begins.

Renovation

Along the river that runs
through the city
new restaurants inaugurate
and cement walkways
with bronze sculptures spring up,
inviting hand-in-hand ambles.
As barges move down river
on hot summer nights
cool jazz draws crowds
and a child from the nearby projects
plays in fountain water.
No one will tell her that
her frolicking is barred,
not on this tangy night
the sun just setting
to the dance of trumpet and sax,
the scent of smoky ribs
wafting over to the couple
settled on the balcony
of their new loft home
in an aged warehouse
the bricks still brawny
       after all this time.

Old Rock and Roll Stars

Aphrodisiac, the memories
of fame. I want you
Baby, I need you.

Give them accolades
these old rockers
still laboring their dance

of what used to be
when their supple bodies
leaped and scored.

I want you, I need you-
       those days of glittering youth.

Three Hearts

My brother, I saw our mother's face
for a crisp moment as if
she were there with us
her love spilling over the sterility

of the room, the steady drip of the IV tube,
the digital monitor with its occasional beep-beep.
My brother, for a transient moment
I saw our mother's face in yours

as you with dread
lay waiting for morning
when the surgeon would open
your proud chest and reach your heart,

its arteries filled with a lifetime of excess.
Too fleeting the shimmer
revealed in the tilt of your head
your eyes becoming her wisdom

a ghostly sifting into the room
from another realm.
Three hearts as one, beating.
We were together again.

Moonflower

Heat shy the bloom that shuns the sun,
Ipomoea albas, a temporal goddess
dodging the noontime kiln.

Wafted from a verdant conclave
a sweet scented circle of pearl,
unfolding its corolla tube,
stamen, and stylus.

From dusk throughout the night,
a summertime

    slow trumpet.

Centenarian

African violets soothed his soul
when his adult son died,
seedlings nurtured through winter
when grey skies prevailed.

A granddaughter, fatherless
he tenderly watched
as for many years he labored on
until again his saddened spirit soared

healed by the sprouting buds
row after row-
a little African violet army!
Then another wife, another life

in riant Florida
but too soon again he was alone,
too frail to grow
his blessed violets

yet rallying for his birthday
when loved ones came from
far away states
to share his frosted cake

flaming with a hundred candles.
His smiling countenance is
commemorated now in fading newsprint-
Local man cultivates prize winning violets.

To the memory of Carl H. Helm
1906-2006

This Tuesday Morning

Warmed by sun
Burly arm of the Oak

Where the squirrel sits
Surveying the feeder

Ripe with suet and seeds
The apron of geraniums

Guarded by gnomes
A stray cat stalking

Percale swinging
On a clothesline

Warmed by sun
      This Tuesday morning.

Oasis

Sun dappled Monarchs bask

On this spot of earth

I've transformed

The fountain water muffles

Sounds of traffic

Beyond the fence,

A barrier to my solitude.

Here I slacken

In the scented flora.

Sometimes I read,

Sometimes I dream

Here in my garden,

Serenity.

Two Haiku

rainwater lingers
in the gutter doves pecking
languid afternoon

a crimson squirrel
makes an autumn question mark
on bark ridged by time

Country Singer

He's edged his craft and added foxy moves
the wide brimmed hat, a pair of boots

toe tapping through twenty years
intermixing oil rig work and bar shows

daring the interest of his wife.
Corralled in jeans snug as a girdle,

beneath strobe lights he struts,
admiring eyes following every twist.

And when he trolls a low note
even the crickets applaud,

while along the stage,
chaste in cellophane dresses,

the roses multiply.

Night in New Orleans

A street wise perfume
of magnolia, bourbon
and dung

rising like steam
from a kettle
the carriage horse clip clopping.

'Tits and twats is what we gots'
calls the hawker,
the bar room door ajar

the passerby glimpsing
bare beasts peering
into the jazzy night.

Stuck in Traffic

Over in the next lane
 sits a guy oblivious
 to her scrutinizing eyes
 crawling past his elbow valley
 climbing up the mountain arm
 crossing the boulder of his shoulder
 hesitating on his noble nose
 where she contemplates,
 Do the lenses hide eyes of blue,
 or another lovely hue?
 Over in the next lane
 he turns and flings to her a grin,
 then shakes his cellular phone in her direction
     mouthing words with perfection-
         What's your number?

Make Over

At the counter a woman
with kohl rimmed eyes

explains the magic of a fluid
available in 24 tints, porcelain to tawny.

Talons painted Eggplant
open the silver top. Lips stained Guava

promise a flawless face-
at $54 an ounce.

Grandma used Vaseline.
But what I most recall

is the vanilla from her pantry
she dabbed behind our ears,

and how we ran through the farm house
giggling, and the scent

      of freshly baked cookies.

Across the Border

Two lovers
In the courtyard
Beneath their sandals
Yellow braids indigo
Monarchs feast on hibiscus
Her perfume vaporizes
In noon day heat
Silvery songs
Squired by trumpets
Blare across the border
On a filigreed bench
        Two lovers.

Tourist

I covet the deep of sleep
Yet city lights saturate my eyes

Creeping down the curtain folds
Divulging the mouse motel

Sticky ready within its belly
The bathroom door ajar,

Where towels ease over
A rod near the tub

And sink side the tumblers are dressed
In their paper frocks.

Reflecting on the note
Signed by Maria

Stating she prepared this room
Especially for me

I await sleep, or morning
While outside this bolted room

Rain softens the boundless night.

Landscaping

Yesterday you planted the chrysanthemum
in the wrong place
although I've cautioned you time and time again:
sun loving plants belong in full sun,
shade lovers in places tinged by shadows.

While I was engaged in other matters,
you dug a hole and plopped it in
atop a handful of peat moss
hand plowed into dark clay.

So proud of yourself to take the initiative
unaware alongside the bleeding heart
I'd planned a glade fern
for that very spot
to unfold into the angel statue.

Frequently we're at odds in various ways.
Your mind aligns floras
into lines of infantrymen
while I see things in random ways.

We all have our schemes
of how things should be.
We all have our dreams.

Summer Night

After you mowed the lawn
and fed the compost heap
we sat on the deck

and surveyed our yard:
turf shorn of its lanky growth
roses and lilies dabbed

from a Monet palette.
We drank margaritas while
night invaded. You lit

a candle and citronella
pierced the grassy night.
Beneath the mesh umbrella

that blurred the moon's face
like a widow's veil
I sipped my salt edged drink.

It was July,
but beyond the flame

     I could sense December.

Oak to Oak

My glimpse from the window
found a neighbor cording a clothes line
Oak to Oak. I watched
as she pinned mama-sized skirts
man-sized Levis, little boy shirts,
and queen-sized sheets
as if that windblown day
she had nothing better to do
than bear a wet burden
basement to backyard
shunning the dryer I know she has,
for drudgery.

Maybe she's concerned
about depleting fossil fuels
or, it could be simply this:
She likes the warm scent
of Spring and Summer
flapping in the wind,
and later a trace of lilacs on the bed
when they make love.

Homemade Lemonade

Seven plump ovals
Of dimpled yellow

Awaiting execution
On the kitchen table

Citric scent swelling the air-
Like summertime.

Reading Marilyn's Mail

Just off Wilshire Boulevard
Beyond the high-rise that pushes the sky

With glass and steel, where the road
Encircles a platter of green

And mausoleum walls make a grey
Barrier to the living,

The blond beauty now rests.
There she is labeled and dated,

Chiseled entry in a registry of stone.
Departed decades, still a legend.

Someone's left a new message
Twist tied to pink carnations.

I lean in to read Marilyn's mail.
You snap my photo, and I muse
    Why does she fascinate us so?

Stormy San Francisco

Just as the sky unburdened
We stepped inside Vesuvio's
And sat in a name-carved booth
Where above, a mural in burnt sienna
Bloomed breasts and buttocks.

Behind the bar a ceramic cat
With red eyes sat on a shelf
By bottles of bourbon and gin,
And upon us conferred his Cheshire grin.

Augmenting the jazzy air,
The scent of books, and cappuccino
Sipped by the old man
Perched on a stool scrawling his muse

In the shadow of Jack Kerouac's alley
Where to the force of thunder
Ghosts of the beat poets clamored.

A Las Vegas Moment

Show girls strutting
with feathers swaying

their red lips framing
flirtatious smiles

descending in elegance
in stiletto heels so thin

prompting me to forego
the buttery escargot

and choose instead
        an undressed salad.

Stopping in Oklahoma City

Crossing America's heart
You behind the wheel
Me, munching whatnot food.

The asphalt artery
Threading cornfields
Illinois into Missouri,

Weaving into blue
The cows and sheep
Billboards that say:
See Jesse James's Cave
Walnut Bowls Ahead.
Not by souvenirs,
Or old hideouts
Our trip detoured
But by a city's shrine:

One hundred, sixty-eight empty chairs
Symbolic of souls taken
        As nearby, the interstate pulsed on.

This Manhattan Morning

Umbrellas diffuse the scent
Of fresh roasted peanuts

As we dodge the man with a broom
Pushing litter from the damp day.

Turning heads at 55th and Broadway
Five dogs on leashes, curtailed by a woman in black

Accents of yellow, the taxis
As drizzle clarifies
               this Manhattan morning.

Revisit to the Old Neighborhood

Leafy canopy thwarting the sun
like a wide brimmed hat.

Too lush, this green of summer
above street and hem.

Once in warmed light
primary colors pedaled this block,

big wheels coiling past saplings
planted by couples

in the vigor of their dreams.
Adorned in updated attire,

sage ranches and tri-levels
hinting adolescent days.

Flash to her heart, the shrub rose
blooming still,
            brighter than she recalls.

Newborn

Big-headed
in a knitted cap,

cocooned in flannel
strewn with yellow bunnies,

tiny fingers curl into
Lilliputian fists and

cuff the talcum scented air as
he roars for Mom

who is lush with love and
sustenance.

For Sale: Canopy Bed

When you got married
I sold your bed
that once held you
with all your teenage secrets.

Beneath the lacy shelter
cross legged, or reclined
you dreamed and solved problems,
mathematical and otherwise.

Still vivid as a cluster of yellow eyed daisies
your memory I passed each day
open door to the vacant room
a challenge to bear.

So when you got married,
I sold your bed.

Before the Pickup

Quiet houses framed by flora
Aproned by weedless lawns.
Parked curbside, recycle bins of orange

Clustered by butterflies and bees
Probed by a man of seasoned years.
Annoying the peace,

He tosses empties into the trunk
With rattles and clinks
      Echoing down the pristine street.

Tableau of Nature

On my walk through the woods
Summer languishes

Like a widow grieving
As grey squirrels entomb acorns

Among the leafy landscape
And the wind hints winter.

Bolting past me and the molting shrubs
A seasonal surprise, the graceful doe-

  Followed by its fawn.

ON WATERLOO ROAD

Not a prized property, pine filled and weedy that
parcel of land, four acres wild on Waterloo Road
my father obtained in lieu of the money
and dreams he lost when the bank failed.

Red dirt and hilly that place abandoned by miners
who hauled away iron ore & left a scooped out gouge
where above, the rocky ledge made a just right place
for fantasies and play. Did you ever tie a thread
around the leg of a June bug? Give it a name, call it
your pet, and let it fly like a tiny kite,
its insect misery a mystery?

Sometimes a careless yank
created a crippled creature.
But with another thread,
 it still could fly, bold green back
 silhouetted against the sky,
like an airplane in turbulence bound
                for an unknown destination.

Trick or Treat Triolet

Last Halloween I saw a clump of grapes, ballooning.
Now. At my door synthetic french fries, fidgeting.

Is this the tot from down the street, so skittish?
Last year I saw a clump of grapes, ballooning.

From sidewalk shadows her daddy hints.
Tiny catsup face daubs a smile & says, *Trick or treat.*

Last Halloween I saw a clump of grapes ballooning.
Now at my door synthetic french fries, fidgeting.

Late November

Fall elaborates
the burning bush
into a crimson hussy

flaming above leaf drift.
Wind tumults past my bay window
swings the Cardinals

snacking at the feeder
forces sunflower seeds
to vacate suet,

tumble onto fescue
succumbing to
snowflakes.
      Winter begins.

Amateur Artist

A Mona Lisa smile graced the woman's face when
mulling her mirrored image

she flecked umber, red and gold
onto her canvas body,

each stroke a flame
elucidating eyes, hair and breasts.

But with the final dab,
she did not recognize herself

a bit Modigliani
this self-portrait in nude

now propped against the Dumpster
where her discarded image will tantalize

the homeless man who in his haze
thinks she is someone
               he once loved.

Siren

Always her slim body
Lures them

To their obsession.
One or more

Accomplices
Made riffraff

By their cravings.
Evicted to sidewalks

Or parking decks
Chronic, as if there's no consequence

When the flame ignites tissue clasping
Their addiction to-

a cigarette.

Cruise Control

Serene as the prairie fields passing,
Fingers rat-a-tatting the wheel.
When I drive I sing

Discordant, my voice a secret
To those in passing cars and trucks.
I could croon my way to Denver

Journey like a long haul driver
Through the landscape of America
End up listening to a poet in Taos

Or watching the bats flee Carlsbad Caverns

       Like a dark shawl
           Flung against the sky.

Mango

Something sensual,
the way you work

this produce the store clerk
rang up as cantaloupe.

Something fervid,
the way you pare

through red blushed skin
to reveal the golden flesh

that clings a seed
like plastic wrap.

From your task
fingers moist

you hand me half
then continue the tussle
       of seed from juicy flesh.

Cocoon

Within
our cotton
cocoon
we knitted
our limbs
into
a perfect fit,
entwining
love
and percale,
dreaming
how
a thousand
years
from now-
someone
found
our
abandoned
shell.

Paradise

There's a candle in white sand
That I light each night and carry out

To where the sea wind on the balcony
Plays with the flame

Like a lover to the surf music.
Tomorrow, I'll scoop alluvium

Mysterious with sea scent
Into an empty bottle

Bury it beneath shorts and jeans
Deep in a suitcase.

These days I'll carry long after
We've left the Mayan sun.

But for tonight again the flame in the wind
Our hearts submerged in love

Like sand hidden seashells.

Slow Poet

Each keyboard click
A labor for that dance
Across my monitor sky

Of high kicking
Black silk words
That fall into a wondrous
Chorus line of metaphors
And similes.
      My muse is poky.

The Only Place Open

Every restaurant
Every supermarket

Is closed tonight.
Even the ethnic eatery

Took a vacation.
The fist of winter

Controls this parking lot
As the lonely

Penguin walk their way
To the shining superstore

Lit like a casino
In the midwestern dark

Selling lots of pizza
This frozen green and red Eve.

Christmas Dinner

Is it Como or Bennett
who sings of snow
and home for Christmas?

Caught in a cradle
of cranberries
the candle gleams
its merry light
on the holiday table.

Unique these moments
wrapped in joy, the scent of food
mingling with the music.

And come next year-
           the joy rephrased returns.

Happy Birthday World

The crescendo
As we blow horns
Drink champagne
Make resolutions
Pink as cotton candy
Temporal as Spring.
Too soon begins
The January surge
Through plate glass
I see raindrops
Presto-
Another year.

About the Author

Irene Sedeora creates both poetry and fiction. Many of her poems and several short stories have appeared in various literary magazines, anthologies & other publications. Sedeora is also the author of the mystery novel, A *Hunting She Did Go.*

In Appreciation

My very special thanks to Ruth Spooner and Rosalie Elkin for their steadfast support, helpful suggestions and enthusiasm for my writing.

▲ ▲ ▲

Poetry is the rhythmical creation
of beauty in words.

Edgar Allan Poe

www.ingramcontent.com/pod-product-compliance
Lightning Source LLC
Chambersburg PA
CBHW071932020426
42331CB00010B/2836